Rhondda Burning

paintings and poems

Robert Havard

Leaf by Leaf is an imprint of Cinnamon Press
www.cinnamonpress.com

The right of Robert Havard to be identified as author of this work has been asserted by him in accordance with the Copyright, Designs and Patent Act, 1988. © 2022, Robert Havard

ISBN 978-1-78864-945-2

British Library Cataloguing in Publication Data. A CIP record for this book can be obtained from the British Library.

All rights reserved. No part of this publication may be reproduced, stored in a retrieval system, or transmitted in any form or by any means, electronic, mechanical, photocopying, recording or otherwise without the prior written permission of the publishers. This book may not be lent, hired out, resold or otherwise disposed of by way of trade in any form of binding or cover other than that in which it is published, without the prior consent of the publishers.

Designed and typeset in Bodoni by Cinnamon Press.

Cinnamon Press is represented by Inpress.

With the steep-sided valley in his visual DNA, Robert Havard has developed a keen relationship between image and poetry over a lifetime of study, teaching and practice. Havard studied with two eye-opening professors, Stephen Reckert and José María Aguirre. He taught at several universities—Cardiff, Los Angeles and Auckland among them—before settling in Aberystwyth where the students and the wide horizons of Cardigan Bay were a joy. On retirement he taught briefly at Bristol and Cardiff, the latter closing a circle begun forty years earlier as an undergraduate,

His images are processed slowly and his first collection came out in his fifties: *Look up without Laughing* (Gomer, 1998).

As Spanish professor he focused on Lorca's generation of poets, several of whom also painted. He learnt from these masters that for both painting and poetry it is the image that focuses the work's power and meaning. He explored this in *The Spanish Eye: Painters and Poets of Spain* (Tamesis, 2007) and it is their interaction that sparks *Rhondda Burning*.

Contents

paintings and poems share the same title except where indicated below

Three Miners / Secrets	9
The Miracle of the Water	11
Soap	13
Smoke	15
Stoned	17
Pantomime of the Eggs	19
Bus	21
The Till	23
Harry the Blind	25
Woman on the Moon	27
Portrait of Gwilym Trefleming Thomas / Lines in Memory of Gwilym Trefleming Thomas	29
Portrait of Ron Berry / Ron	31
Rhondda Burning	33
After the fight	35
Man on a Bench	37
Stone	39
The Stone Bridge	41
Gordon in the Black	43
Whale	45
Are You with the Environment?	47
Pregnant Women playing Snooker near the Llŷn	49
Belchite	51
The Stone of Madness	53
On Bardsey	55
The Wrasse	57
Tom	59
Squiggles	61
River	63
Endnotes	64
Painting sizes	65

In memory of my parents Ann and Gwilym Havard

Rhondda Burning

Secrets

It was a secret where they went
and a secret what they did all day.
We'd see them come back on our streets
—white teeth, eyes white—in an eruption
of spit and smoke, like they owned the place.
But they owned nothing, those who scoured
the pavement for lumps in their gob,
those whose backs broke in sagging beds.
Cold mornings we'd hear the hooter
and the tramp of boots off to war.
But paupers they were, not heroes.
That was the worst kept secret: dogs
of the earth, mugs we'd say, expendable.
They didn't own the dust in their lungs.

The Miracle of the Water

The last fortnight in July
Jesus touched the river's pulse
and said, suddenly. 'Be clean'.
I came down with my jam jar
from the tall church on the hill
and watched the clouds wiping soot
from the water's calloused toes.
Then I saw all the fish had
gone, aye, off to Trecco Bay
with 5000 miners' boys.

Soap

I didn't know a crib from a gob, a stall
from a heading, pneumoconiosis
from silicosis, but I'd heard the tramp
of boots and tired hymns, seen the sky blue stains
on gaunt faces, silverfish disgorging
in gratings, and once, calling on a pal,
I saw a tin bath by the fire floating
wreaths of soap, pants and bra dumped alongside,
and I heard a rasping for air upstairs,
then softly: '… He's gone to the pictures, boy'.

Smoke

To reach the mountain you ran a gauntlet, a blind
hoot-hoofing charge up iron steps into shrouds of sail
that smut your eyes and pit your throat. Head down, you groped
a rail, sleeve, grille, belching funnels ripping your ear-
drums and forty tribes of chockfull wagons—*beedoo
beedoo*-clanking their anthracite chorus through plank
gaps underfoot, all shiny wet as the same speed,
same colour—*beedoobeedoo*—river going down
and out, always out. A blast of steam, juddering
points, and your eyes went white, your nose acrid again,
and there you fell, coughing your lungs onto coarse grass.
This black exodus, this grey detritus, wagon
after slow wagon carting off the glint, dumping
dullard slag. Only the mountain stood back, rock hard
and free as ferns, trapping clouds in the Basin. Then
a shrill whistle; the smoke cleared, and it too had gone.

Stoned

Thor's missiles cluster-bombed
inside my head and we two
ricocheted to a clattering stop.
Khrushchev…? A mine gone bang…
or had he crashed the car again?
Before I knew it he was through his door,
fists flying after runaway urchins.
One stood back eyeballing me
on chip-stones by the Council gate.
As I took him in, a last handful
detonated the only car in the street.

Pantomime of the Eggs

It looked safe enough in your hand, wedged in your palm
by that stout thumb like a cloud stuck in the Basin.
Your fingertips said different: they fidgeted
the enemy shell and told the odds against cracking
on the rim, not in the pan, the oh-so delicate
membrane crunch and the yoke's headlong gravity.
Also the recriminations, which fizzed hard in
the albumen, so no one knew if it was fat egos
or eggs in fat that kicked off the morning riot.

Bus

Kept in, I caught a service bus
home: nine miles, changing at Pandy
where I climb metal stairs and sit
among sullen men hunched forward
on their way to work. No one speaks
above the bus din, but dust shifts
in jags of sunlight when someone
coughs or blows smoke on the donkey
jacket in front. Brash, I light up
in solidarity.
                These men,
anonymous in their work clothes,
strangers all to me, readying
themselves in mute conspiracy
for the penal shift, doing what
they do, out of sight, underground,
the smell of dark already thick
on them.
           Streets inch by in failing
light: John, Chrichton, Stuart… roll-calling
that master of detention who'd
not set foot on Bute Square. My stop.

The Till

It was tucked away at the back of the shop, under white
clouds overlooking the river, its wood bleached, its bell long
silent. There behind frosted glass went the takings, the count
of a morning or a day selling shoes. Out came half-crowns,
ten-bob notes, thru'penny bits of change, as fingers pressed coin
easy as winking from skin-smooth slots into a closed palm.
The woman who watched it with a wrinkle of maths on her mind
liked to quip: 'Can't take it with you, the money not the shoes!'
Her frown stiffened under strip lighting when the bell was fixed
and a lined roll put in so all sales could be inked in red,
down to a pair of laces.
                                  On Thursdays, half-day closing,
when a boy came off the school bus with his throat in splinters,
stub fingers dipped behind frosted glass and only the clouds
on the river witnessed him pick enough stones to head down
Bracchi's and say in a breath: 'Five, Cam, 'n box of matches'.

Harry the Blind

The signpost outside our shop had a big
Y on it showing the road split further
up at Penpych and every now and then
a double-decker would smack *Blaenrhondda*
right behind *Blaencwm* like a wet *Echo*.
One fine day some bright spark on the Council
had the post moved two feet in from the kerb
without telling Harry the Blind who played
honkytonk Wednesday nights to cider-heads
in the Stuart. So Harry came down Bute
Street shops whistling a favourite tune he didn't
(*smack!*) play that Wednesday, or again, ever.

Woman on the Moon

It's early hours and the screen flickers
with the ghosts of conquering heroes
who plant their single flag in ashes
they might have raised in Hiroshima.

I see the round line of the horizon
pale against the night's haunted space,
and nearer to me another curve
of one who sleeps through this history.

No one is there to hail them, no one
bends his neck to the vanquished floor,
but millions see a stiff flag stand
to salute us in the windless air.

My Venus stirs as earthly voices
outdo each other's animation.
When she excuses her tiredness
I know my astronaut days are gone.

20. vii. 1969

Lines in Memory of
Gwilym Trefleming Thomas

At first light, on Bute Square,
a hooter and the tramp of boots:
comrades in arms, without guns.

That first shift off the farm:
air down Lady Margaret, up Bute shaft,
kept the dust off your lungs.

Hundred percent, you gave and got;
hundred percent, scarce a day lost.
Dram for dram, in a four-foot run,
fills an ocean.

Semaphore eyes see in the dark;
your forehead, pockmarked with calamities;
that nose, catacombs of erosion.

Black boots, white scarf,
laced and buttoned for all eventualities.
You were gone, Gwilym,
before the canary choked.

Above St Mary's, the language is ripe.
At the hairpin, they gob on scratchings of grass, resigned.

You walk home,
the moon on Cwm Saerbren;
stump of kindling under one arm,
magnolia on the breeze from your garden.

Tin bath by the fire, scrubber ready, no hymn.
Go down the pub, Gwilym.
Trevor will fetch you up.

Big moon on Tydraw: your face in fire-glow.
On the hearth, flames in a pint glass.

You come and go,
between pipe-smoke and pipe-smoke:
lungfuls squeezed out slow as a pit-pony's fart.

You clear your throat, the grate sizzles;
smack your lips, the room smiles back.

Say what you like, Dai Morris was always in the game…
But that man, Hain…
Talk fades:
you stare, unseeing, at wallpaper stains.

What comes, Gwilym, breathless, in the shadow?
Senghenydd, Cambrian, Aberfan…
a boy in a barrow?

Fifty years down the line
you wonder was it all worthwhile.
Somewhere, underground,
a drip of water resounds.

Ron

You didn't suffer jibes about compo,
a hard day's shift, or Rene's weak bladder
that kept her all day in Treherbert loo.
Not without eyeballing the smart-arse
who'd sup his pint sharpish and slink off.
And if some Bloomsbury slickhead twanged
he'd fetch secateurs to your typescript,
he got the same hard stare down the phone.
So *Roots* joined them in your bottom drawer
and off you charged up forestry tracks
after peregrines in the Reliant,
your front wheel digging its own rut.

Rhondda Burning

Boys are out late tonight
on Penrhys, Pandy and Bute mountain,
every *twmp* and *gnol* alight:
Rhondda burning, burning, burning…

Squirrels once went tree to tree
from Blaencwm to Pontypridd.
Now there's not a single leaf
falls on Bwlch or Penpych:
Rhondda burning, burning, burning…

When the last collier died
a hooter sounded in the mine.
Tonight a widow wonders why
dawn breaks on four sides:
Rhondda burning, burning, burning…

Did testosterone
torch the world tonight
or were these fires
fuelled by spite?
Rhondda burning, burning, burning…

See the fires rage all night
on Penrhys, Pandy and Bute mountain,
every *twmp* and *cwm* alight:
Rhondda burning, burning, burning…

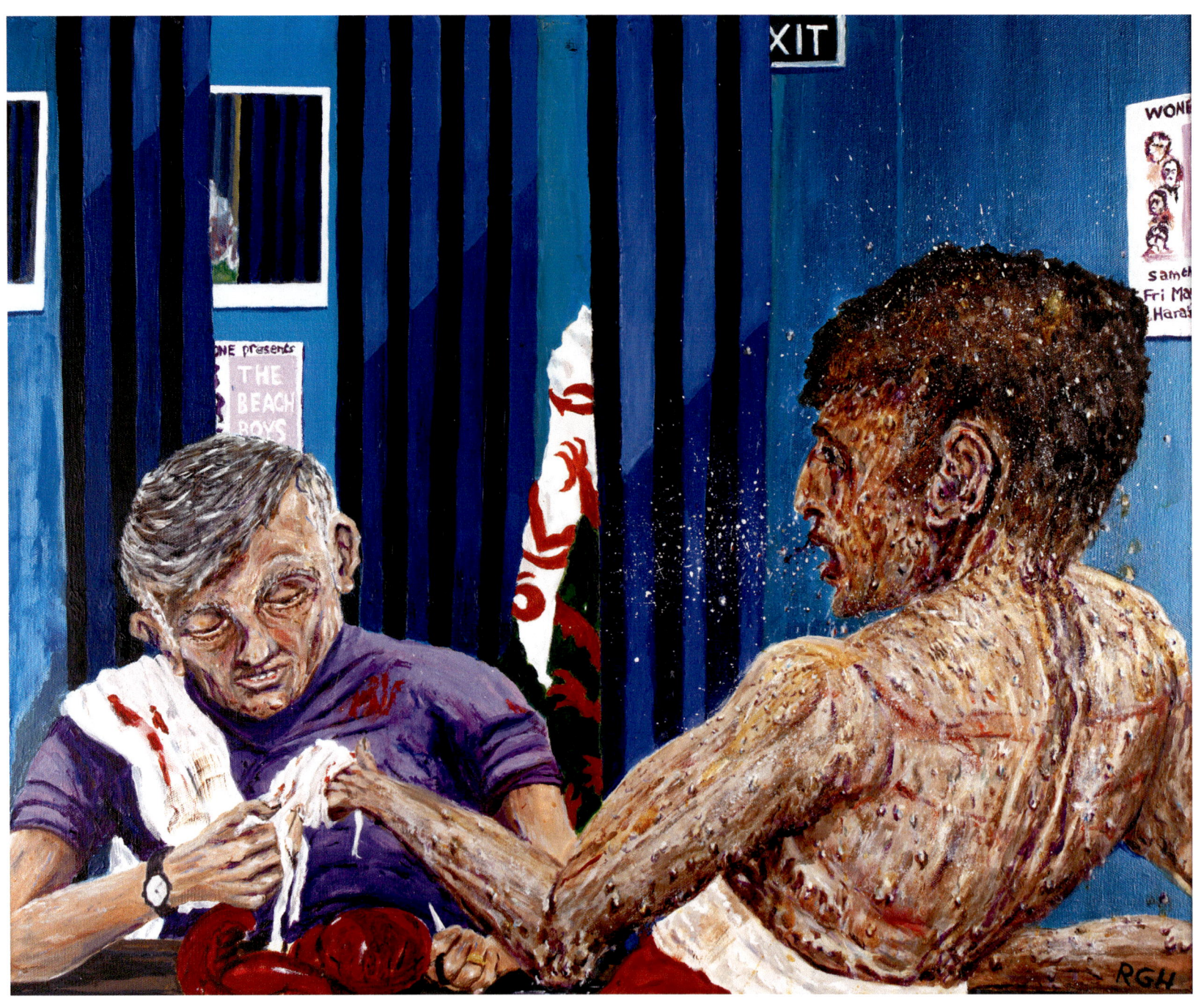

After the fight

'Done good, didn' I, Eddie…?'
                        'Real good, boy, till the eighth.'
'Showed him a thing or two about boxing, didn' I, Eddie…?'
                        'You showed him all right.'
'Stuck on the end of my jab he was like jam…'
                        'Strawberry his face was, aye.'
'Couldn' lay a finger on me, could he, Eddie…?'
                        'Not a glove, boy.'
'Swatting air he was, then one lucky…'
                        'One lucky punch that was coming all night.'

Man on a Bench

I like this bench.
It's do-able
in short steps
and long pauses.
I sit my arse down,
roll a fat fag,
fill my lungs,
and the village
disappears
in smoke and pines.

Stone

It has a presence this stone, an aura
of stillness that inundates the clearing
and anchors you to its primitive bulk.
Cathedral white, mottled in what appears
the droppings of an ancient bird, its deep
fissures and irregular protrusions
invite speculation on a past life.
Overhead, branches cast moving shadows
that darken the cranium of an old man
who stands mute before the phenomenon.

The Stone Bridge

Thought he was taking the Michael I did
when he said: 'You got the stone colour there
bang on.'
        'White, you mean?' I asked, cap-in-hand.
Pointing at liquid highlights, he spoke
his last words on my *breakthrough* show at Bear
Steps Gallery: 'White, that's it…'
                        Housed I was,
in fact, in the 'attic space', twelve airy
steps higher than most Shrewsbury art buffs
were wont to tread. I saw him then, smirking
at me from *terra firma*, which made no
sense either.
           So, Smart Pants, I squirt *Tits White*
straight out of my tube, do I? Back I turned
to the pile and—Smack!—the stones hit me *un*,
deux, trois, quatre pommes de Cézanne right between
the eyes. *Merde, Monsieur!* Did I do that? *Mmwwhuhh…!*

Gordon in the Black

You hold the glass well
early evening,
sidling a full pint
safe to your table,
Michelle watching
for slips and slops.
Soon she'll ask something
to keep you at the bar
a sip or two longer,
then nod you to your stool.

Whale

Twenty foot long, twelve tonnes heavy,
he'd been dead at sea for weeks
before beaching on Ynyslas sand.
Young finback or full grown minke,
he stank the air: head and flukes torn,
baleen holed, penis now a doleful
protrusion under a brindled belly.
Ceredigion Council were hoping
a spring tide would lift his carcass
across the Dyfi to save burial costs.

24. xii. 2015

Are You with the Environment?

The camera round my neck got his
ackers up, I could tell. What was I
doing poking my nose in, snapping
zinc mess and that? Next I'd be telling
him what to eat, drink, how to roof
his house, he shouldn't wonder. Bugger
Europe! We've all got indoor toilets
now. What's wrong with Welsh slate?
Beats me, I said, dust in my throat.

Pregnant Women playing Snooker near the Llŷn

Being in the club has its perks:
fresh air, plenty of stretching,
a cool baize taking the weight off
your belly and tender parts.
Best of all, no innuendos and no
shilling in the light under a full moon.

Belchite

This blue Aragon sky brings tears to the eye.
All over town shells rain down.

And you, Tom Picton, all those years ago,
were you stood on this same spot,
wondering where the hell you were
and why it was so hot?

Between somewhere and somewhere else, they said,
hard to find on a map, arguing the toss,
spouting crap, that bell ringing in my head.

A guard smacked his gun on another prisoner's head,
so you laid him out in the sun and next thing you were dead.

Fighting, fighting, fighting, under this blue Aragon sky.
Fighting, fighting, fighting, the only way to live or die.

The Stone of Madness

Salvador the second and only son,
risen from the ashes of the beloved first one,
you had to own your own life before you could walk,
dumping on the bed, stairs, front-door mat,
shushing night whispers with googie-talk.

Papá's dread of the pox bequeathed a pygmy cock.
Mamá fled germs and found paranoia
in the confessional box. You, afeared of women,
took for a wife the biggest Paris tart,
Gala—*sic* Alba for Goya—hailed her the Virgin
soulmate of your life, untouchable as a fart.

You loved Federico, his dark olive skin,
but his gypsy eyes made yours go dim.
Quixote showed you how to tie the world
to your whim, with a flick of the wrist
when no one was looking. Hieronymus how
to paint your insides out in clear brush-strokes
without crossing the line. A bulb from your head
was all it took, laid flat on the table, hard-edged
as a stick of bread.

On Bardsey

Wading ashore, I tread the bones of saints
and whales, the tide oscillating between
ebb and flow with each new wave. Marram grass
leads me to a bank where octopus legs
lie drab as drumsticks in a supermarket.
Here, under a seal's nose, on wood washed smooth
as flesh, your ankle is so well sculpted
I have to get down on my knees and pray.

The Wrasse

I held it in my hand
at the end of the jetty,
tender as a lover
in the fold of my palm,
transclucent as the sea
against the still sand.

Tom

Good nights you trod the Old Vic boards
with Gielgud vowels sharp as swords.
Back in Llanon, you soliloquized
like Prospero, when a neap tide
caught you cold. At ninety-four,
you hit a stone, crashed your bike
and broke your nose. How you got up
to strut your stuff, heaven knows.

Squiggles

Look again.
Harder this time.
What do you see
in the sand, salt, sky?

What brings you back here?

A gull's squawk,
the soughing wind,
the prospect of a message
in the squiggles?

If squiggles they be.

River

It must have happened in the night,
when nesting birds lay heavy with sleep.
They woke, like me, and shook their wings,
startled by the river's crystal light:
the rocks, mountain, sky and ferns
all there, lustred on a satin sleeve.

Something told me this moment was mine
to keep. When age comes to ache my bones,
tremors of subsidence shudder my soul,
I'll sail away, in my turn,
fly to the mountain like a bird:
this air, this water, my mother lode.

Endnotes

'Three Miners': draws on American photo-journalist Eugene Smith's renowned shot, *Three Miners at Coedely*, published in *Life* magazine in 1950.

'Ron Berry': ex-miner and acclaimed writer (1920-97) from Blaencwm, Treherbert, two of whose novels, *So Long, Hector Bebb* and *Flame and Slag*, are in the prestigious Library of Wales series (2006 and 2012). *Roots* remains unpublished.

'Rhondda Burning': on 27 March 2017 several fires were lit simultaneously on different Rhondda hillsides, rendering fire-fighters powerless to stop flames reaching towards the houses. Mountain fires were a valley tradition, but synchronizing them was new.

'After the Fight': Eddie Avoth, born Cardiff 1945, fought Mike Quarry in a final eliminator for the world cruiserweight title in Los Angeles, 6 June 1970. I went to the fight in LA where I was living at the time and, having previously met Avoth in Wales, paid my respects afterwards in the loser's dressing-room.

'Belchite': lies in its ruins as a monument to the Spanish Civil War. Tom Picton was one of four Treherbert miners who fought in Spain. He saw action in the First World War, returned to the mines, was a booth-fighter and so-called mountain-fighter. Picton bears the distinction of being the only foreign POW to be executed in Franco's jails.

'The Stone of Madness': Hieronymus Bosch's painting, *Extraction of the Stone of Madness*, depicts the often fatal operation of trepanning performed in medieval times in an attempt to cure a deranged mind. Salvador Dalí, whose own art practice centred on what he called his Paranoiac-critical method, was familiar with this and other works by El Bosco in the Prado Museum, which he frequented as a student in Madrid. Here Dalí takes the role of surgeon and his wife Gala sits where a nun sat in the original. 'Federico' is the poet García Lorca who was executed by fascists at the outbreak of the Civil War in Spain in July 1936.

'On Bardsey': the island at the tip of the Llŷn Peninsula in north-west Wales—Ynys Enlli in Welsh, 'island in the stream'. A centre for bards and pilgrims, three trips to this 'island of 20,000 saints' counted as one to the Holy Land on the salvation ledger.

Painting sizes

(in inches)

Three Miners (20 x 30)
The Miracle of the Water (30 x 20)
Soap (40 x 30)
Smoke (36 x 24)
Stoned (54 x 18)
Pantomime of the Eggs (36 x 24)
Bus (40 x 30)
The Till (24 x 30)
Harry the Blind (24 x 35)
Woman on the Moon (30 x 20)
Portrait of Gwilym Trefleming Thomas (12 x 16)
Portrait of Ron Berry (12 x 16)
Rhondda Burning (48 x 16)
After the Fight (30 x 24)
Man on a Bench (16 x 20)
Stone (16 x 12)
The Stone Bridge (20 x 16)
Gordon in the Black (24 x 30)
Whale (24 x 20)
Are you with the Environment? (26 x 18)
Pregnant Women Playing Snooker near the Llŷn (26 x18)
Belchite (20 x 16)
The Stone of Madness (12 x 18)
On Bardsey (16 x 12)
Tom (12 x16)
The Wrasse (16 x 12)
Squiggles (16 x 12)
River (48 x 24)